FRANCISCAN MISSION ARCHITECTURE OF CALIFORNIA

by

Rexford Newcomb

from the Library of Blake Konegal

DOVER PUBLICATIONS, INC.
NEW YORK

Published in Canada by General Publishing Company, Ltd., 30 Lesmill Road, Don Mills, Toronto,
Ontario.

Published in the United Kingdom by Constable
and Company, Ltd., 10 Orange Street, London
WC 2.

This Dover edition, first published in 1988, is a
republication of the unabridged and corrected edition
first published by Dover in 1973 under the title *The
Franciscan Mission Architecture of Alta California*.
The work was originally published under that title by
The Architectural Book Publishing Company, New
York, in 1916. The illustrations were renumbered for
the 1973 Dover edition.

International Standard Book Number: 0-486-25838-6
Library of Congress Catalog Card Number: 72-80877

Manufactured in the United States of America
Dover Publications, Inc.
31 East 2nd Street
Mineola, New York 11501

PREFACE

IN studying the sources of design in architecture, it is seldom that a chance is given to Americans to examine the original buildings themselves without crossing the water, and among the limited sources within our own boundaries there is no class of buildings more interesting than the missions built in the Southwest by the monks of the Franciscan Order. So many elements combine themselves in these buildings that the architect can find among them precedents for the design of a church, a school, a residence, a workshop, or, if he desires, all of these well connected and charmingly related.

The purpose of the writer in making the present series of studies was to assist, in a practical way, the cause of architecture by recording by means of notes, drawings and photographs, the real spirit and detail of these buildings, so well adapted and appropriate to the land of their inception, before the last vestige of the buildings themselves had disappeared from the earth. The writer was convinced that many architects were designing in the style who had never seen a mission, and that many more were designing in the style who, if they had ever seen the old buildings, were making poor interpretation of the spirit in which they were erected.

The study has extended over four years, during which time the author has made accurate and detailed drawings, sketches and photographs of the existing ruins. In connection with this research he is under obligation to many students in his classes for help in making the surveys and especially to his photographers, Messrs. Putnam and Valentine of Los Angeles, for many favors rendered and efficient labors performed.

The plates and photographs are almost self-explanatory. The letters in script on the various plates were copied from manuscript books to be found now in the various old mission libraries and represent, quite as much as the building details, the thought and spirit of the padres. It is believed that the plates, although not exhaustive, represent a fairly well-rounded series for use in architects' offices and it is hoped that they will fill that need so clearly apparent at the present time.

Long Beach, California   REXFORD NEWCOMB
June 1, 1916

HISTORICAL NOTE

WHILE our forefathers were building fast and strong the foundations of our national life upon the eastern coast and expressing that love for liberty and freedom in a free use of the Georgian style, those pioneers of the West, the soldiers and sailors of old Spain, together with the padres of the Franciscan Order, were conquering the country of the Pacific for Christ and the crown. The buildings erected by these padres express, in a similar manner, the culture and civilization that they heralded in the land and are no less interesting and just as important architecturally and historically as the Colonial of the Atlantic Seaboard.

To be sure, these old buildings do not represent the same variety of design or elaborateness of detail found in the more populous cities of Mexico or even in Texas and Arizona, yet they stand as concrete reminders of Spanish occupation and admirable examples of buildings conceived in the style and manner appropriate to the country in which they were built. And thus far they command the attention and respect of all architects and designers of the present day and offer many fine suggestions for modern buildings with similar requirements.

Alta California of the Spanish days extended from San Diego on the south to Sonoma, just beyond San Francisco Bay, on the north, and this stretch of coast land, something over five hundred miles in length, was covered by a chain of mission establishments, situated about a day's journey apart along the old coast trail known as El Camino Real (the Royal Road). The first mission was established at San Diego in 1769 by Father Junípero Serra, president of the missions; the second, San Carlos, was located on Monterey Bay in 1770, while the intervening territory was covered as years went on, so that by 1823 the chain of twenty-one missions, together with several asistencias, or contributing chapels, was complete. A complete list of the establishments with their dates of foundation is given herewith. The locations may be determined on the map, Plate I.

1	Mission	San Diego de Alcalá	July	16, 1769
2	"	San Carlos de Monterey	June	3, 1770
3	"	San Antonio de Padua	July	14, 1771
4	"	San Gabriel Arcángel	Sept.	8, 1771
5	"	San Luis Obispo de Tolosa	Sept.	1, 1772
6	"	San Francisco de Asís	Oct.	9, 1776
7	"	San Juan Capistrano	Nov.	1, 1776

8	Mission	Santa Clara de Asís	Jan. 18, 1777
9	"	San Buenaventura	Mar. 21, 1782
10	"	Santa Barbara	Dec. 4, 1786
11	"	La Purísima Concepción	Dec. 8, 1787
12	"	Santa Cruz	Aug. 28, 1791
13	"	Nuestra Señora de La Soledad	Oct. 9, 1797
14	"	San José	June 11, 1797
15	"	San Juan Bautista	June 24, 1797
16	"	San Miguel Arcángel	July 25, 1797
17	"	San Fernando, Rey de España	Sept. 8, 1797
18	"	San Luis, Rey de Francia	June 13, 1798
19	"	Santa Inés	Sept. 17, 1804
20	"	San Rafael Arcángel	Dec. 14, 1817
21	"	San Francisco de Solano	April 25, 1823

Of course the purpose of the establishments was to Christianize and civilize the Indian population and to this end each mission establishment was in charge of two priests, one of whom superintended the manual labors, the teaching of the arts, and managed the farm, while the other attended to the spiritual needs and book learning of the Indians. The education of the Indian was of two kinds, namely: training in the various occupations and crafts like weaving, tanning, shoe-making, grain, fruit and cattle raising, and the book learning such as the Spanish language, Christian doctrine and singing.

The daily routine at any one of the missions was something of the following nature: The Angelus at sunrise called the Indians who lived about the mission to assembly in the chapel, where they were required to attend morning prayers and mass and receive religious instruction. After mass breakfast was served, after which all went to their work. At eleven o'clock dinner was eaten, after which they rested until 2 P. M., when work was resumed and continued until an hour before sunset, when the Angelus bell was rung again. After prayers and the rosary, the evening meal was eaten and the Indians were free to dance or indulge in any other harmless amusement.

The young Indian women were not allowed to reside in the family huts, but were kept in a convent under the charge of a trusted Indian matron, who was responsible for their welfare and education in the crafts. They were not allowed to leave the convent until they had been won by Indian youths and were ready to marry. The courtship took place through the barred window as in Spain and Mexico. After marriage they settled down in a hut among the other Indian families.

The missions, in addition to great fields, pastures for sheep, cattle and horse raising and gardens for vegetables, had rose and flower gardens and orchards of fruit. Flour mills were operated at several missions, in some cases by water. Irrigation was practised and elaborate dams and flumes of masonry are still extant to vouch for their engineering ability. In several cases fountains were supplied with running water from the mountains, as were great washing vats and bath houses.

To meet the requirements placed upon it the building for a mission must be especially designed. Since there were no architects in the country and few, if any, artisans (usually craftsmen of any variety had to be brought from Mexico), the padres themselves were obliged to design and superintend the construction of the buildings. The mission system required, first of all of course, a church, then priests' quarters, shops for workmen, servants' and soldiers' quarters, convent for the young women, guest rooms, store rooms, refectory, kitchen, etc. The priests must have supervision and access at all times and the establishment must be capable of protection from attacks from without. Hence the arrangement around an open court or patio seemed the solution. This is the plan of all missions that had any pretensions at all. The patio served a very utilitarian purpose and at the same time had an admirable artistic purpose in unifying the plan. In case of attack from without all could be gathered into the patio for protection, and in the hey-day of the mission period (1800 to 1822) the patio at any mission presented, no doubt, an appearance, ever, of vari-colored activity. On the plan of San Juan Capistrano, Plate 15, will be noted the relation of the patio to the general mission layout. It will be seen that here was the centre of mission private life, while the plaza was the centre of community social life. On the plaza were located the priests' quarters, soldiers' quarters, refectory, guest-rooms and offices, while the servants' quarters, refectory, kitchen, larders, storehouses and shops flanked the patio.

The features that characterize the style may be summarized as follows:
1. Patio plan with garden or fountain.
2. Solid and massive walls, piers and buttresses.
3. Arched corridors.
4. Curved, pedimented gables.
5. Terraced bell-towers, with dome and lantern.
6. Pierced belfries.
7. Wide, projecting eaves.
8. Broad, undecorated, wall surfaces.
9. Low, sloping, red-tile roofs.

Examples of these characteristics are shown by photograph and drawing. Several selections from the Arizonian variety of the style have been included for comparative purposes.

In conclusion, it can be said that these buildings exhibit unusually fine proportions, obtained in spite of poor materials, lack of skilled workmen and rude implements. In view of the fact that these buildings were designed by laymen, it seems wonderful that such charming results should have been obtained.

LIST OF PLATES

FRANCISCAN
MISSION ARCHITECTURE
OF CALIFORNIA

PLATE I

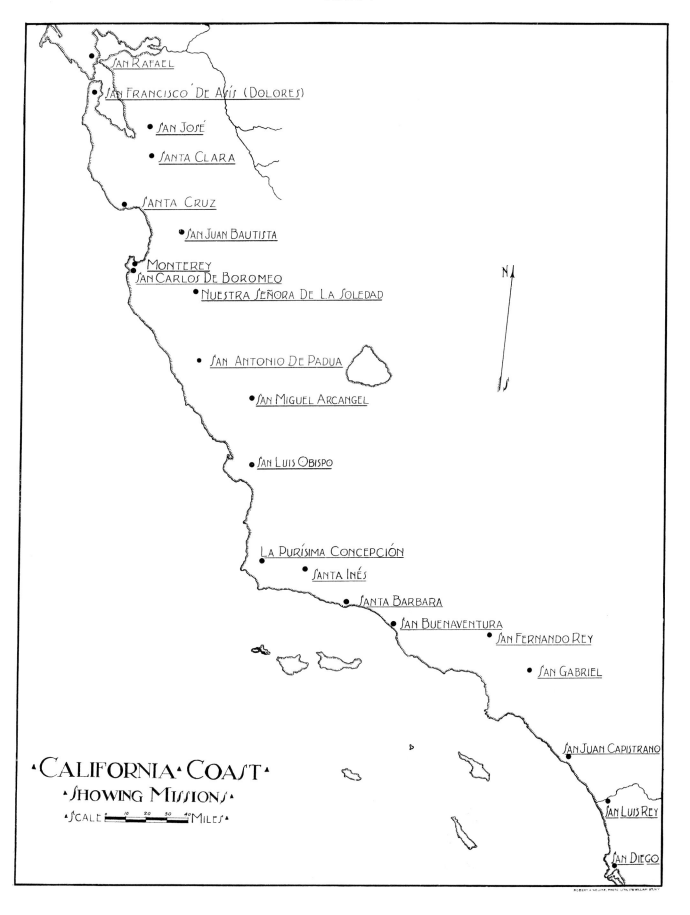

San Rafael

San Francisco De Asís (Dolores)

San José

Santa Clara

Santa Cruz

San Juan Bautista

Monterey
San Carlos De Boromeo

Nuestra Señora De La Soledad

San Antonio De Padua

San Miguel Arcangel

N

S

San Luis Obispo

La Purísima Concepción

Santa Inés

Santa Barbara

San Buenaventura

San Fernando Rey

San Gabriel

San Juan Capistrano

·CALIFORNIA·COAST·
·SHOWING MISSIONS·
·SCALE 0 10 20 30 40 MILES·

San Luis Rey

San Diego

ROBERT A. WELCKE, PHOTO-LITH. 176 WILLIAM ST. N.Y.

PLATE 2

La Purísima Concepción

PLATE 3

San Miguel Arcángel—Corridor

PLATE 4

San Juan Bautista

PLATE 5

San Juan Bautista

PLATE 6

San Antonio de Padua

PLATE 7

San Antonio de Padua—Ruined Church

PLATE 8

San Xavier del Bac, Arizona—Façade

PLATE 9

San Xavier del Bac, Arizona—Church and Interior

PLATE 10

San Carlos de Monterey—Façade and Detail of Façade

PLATE II

San Carlos (Carmel) —Church

PLATE 12

San Carlos (Carmel)—Façade

PLATE 13

San Carlos (Carmel)—Campanile

PLATE 14

San Carlos (Carmel)—Font

PLATE 15

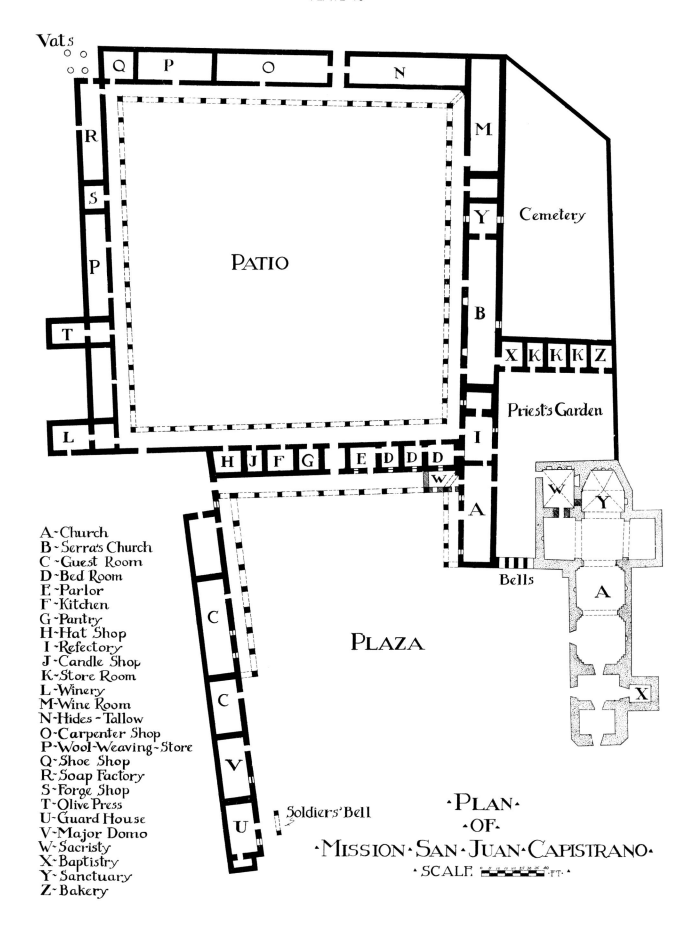

Vats

Q P O N

R
S
P
T
L

PATIO

M
Y
B
X K K K Z
I
A

Cemetery

Priest's Garden

W Y

A

X

Bells

H J F G E D D D
W

PLAZA

C

C

V

U

Soldiers' Bell

A~Church
B~Serra's Church
C~Guest Room
D~Bed Room
E~Parlor
F~Kitchen
G~Pantry
H~Hat Shop
I~Refectory
J~Candle Shop
K~Store Room
L~Winery
M~Wine Room
N~Hides~Tallow
O~Carpenter Shop
P~Wool~Weaving~Store
Q~Shoe Shop
R~Soap Factory
S~Forge Shop
T~Olive Press
U~Guard House
V~Major Domo
W~Sacristy
X~Baptistry
Y~Sanctuary
Z~Bakery

·PLAN·
·OF·
·MISSION·SAN·JUAN·CAPISTRANO·
·SCALE· 0 5 10 15 20 25 30 35 40 ·FT·

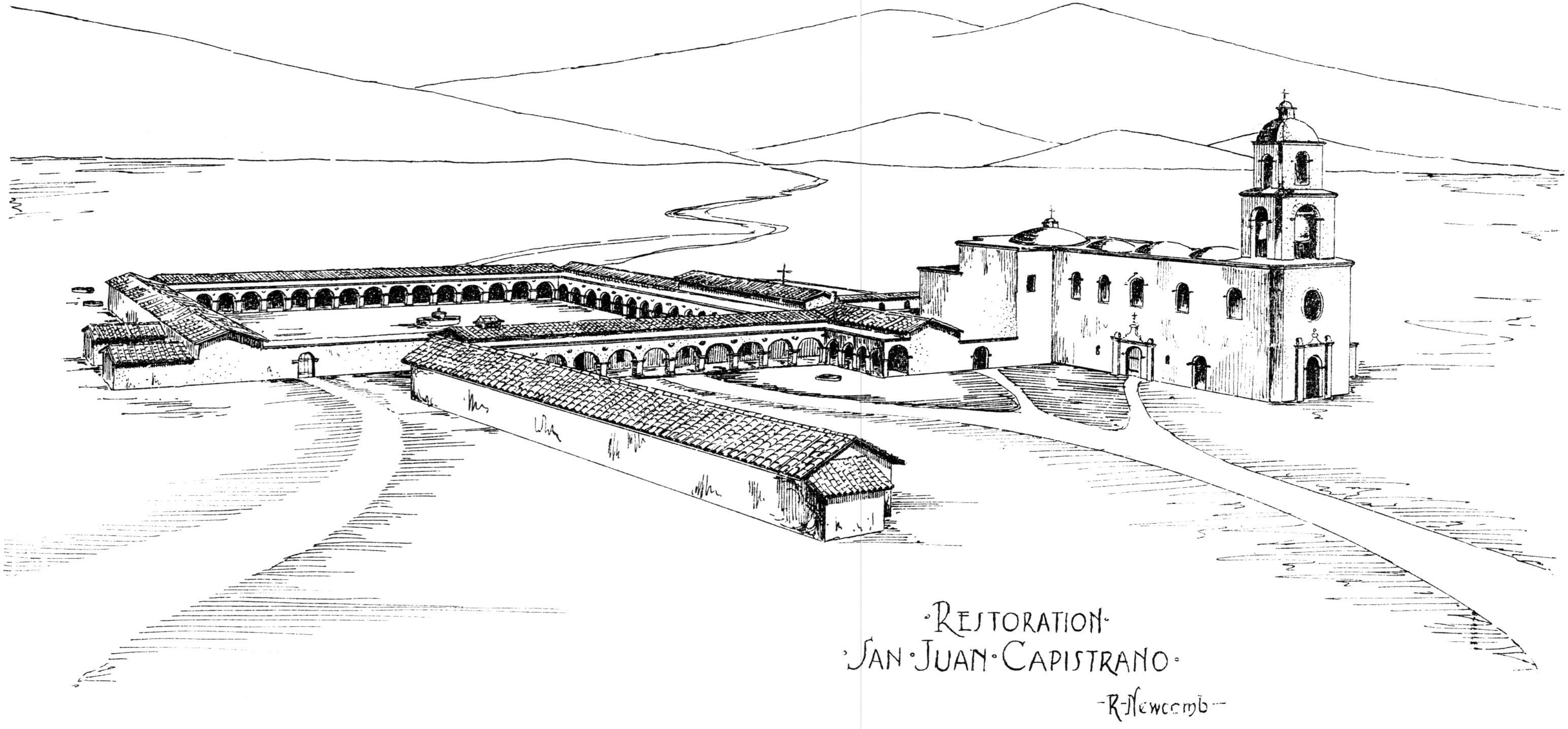

PLATE 16

·RESTORATION·
·SAN·JUAN·CAPISTRANO·
—R·Newcomb—

PLATE 17

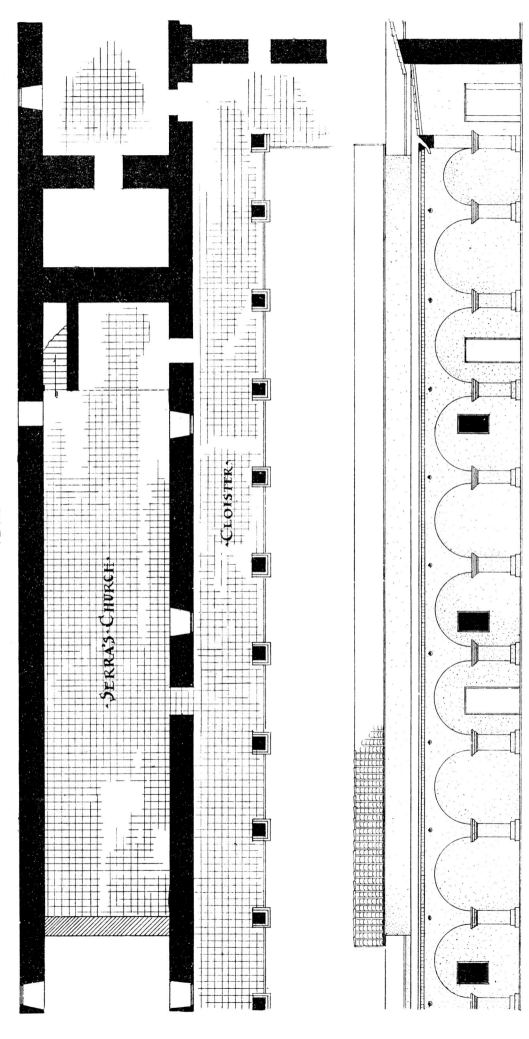

·PATIO·
·SAN·JUAN·CAPISTRANO·
·SCALE· FT·

PLATE 18

San Juan Capistrano—Front Corridors

PLATE 19

San Juan Capistrano—Ruined Arches

PLATE 20

San Juan Capistrano—Plaza, Looking Toward Present Chapel

PLATE 21

San Juan Capistrano—Ruined Sanctuary

PLATE 22

San Juan Capistrano—Doorway in Sanctuary

PLATE 23

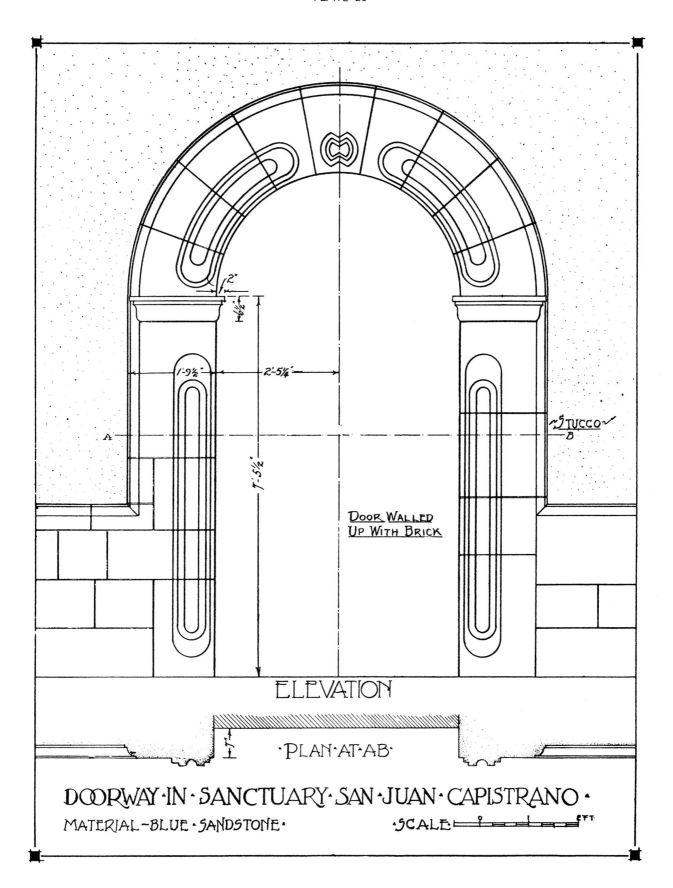

2"

1'6½"

1'9½"

2'-5¼"

A   STUCCO   B

1'-5½"

DOOR WALLED
UP WITH BRICK

ELEVATION

1"

·PLAN·AT·AB·

DOORWAY·IN·SANCTUARY·SAN·JUAN·CAPISTRANO·

MATERIAL—BLUE·SANDSTONE·   ·SCALE·⊢─────┼─────┼─────┤ 2FT

PLATE 24

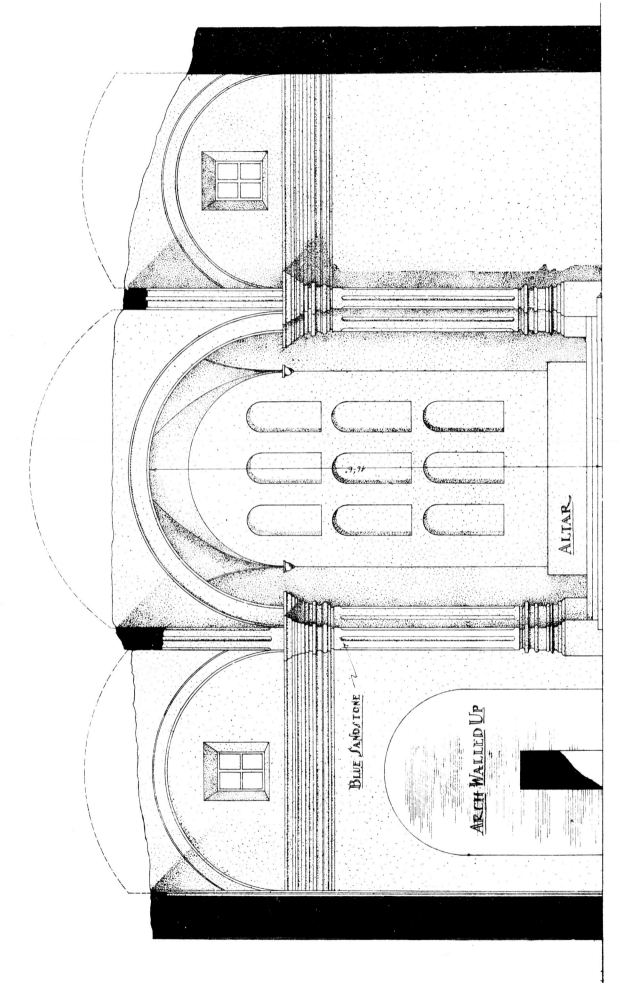

San Juan Capistrano—Section at Transept, Elevation

PLATE 25

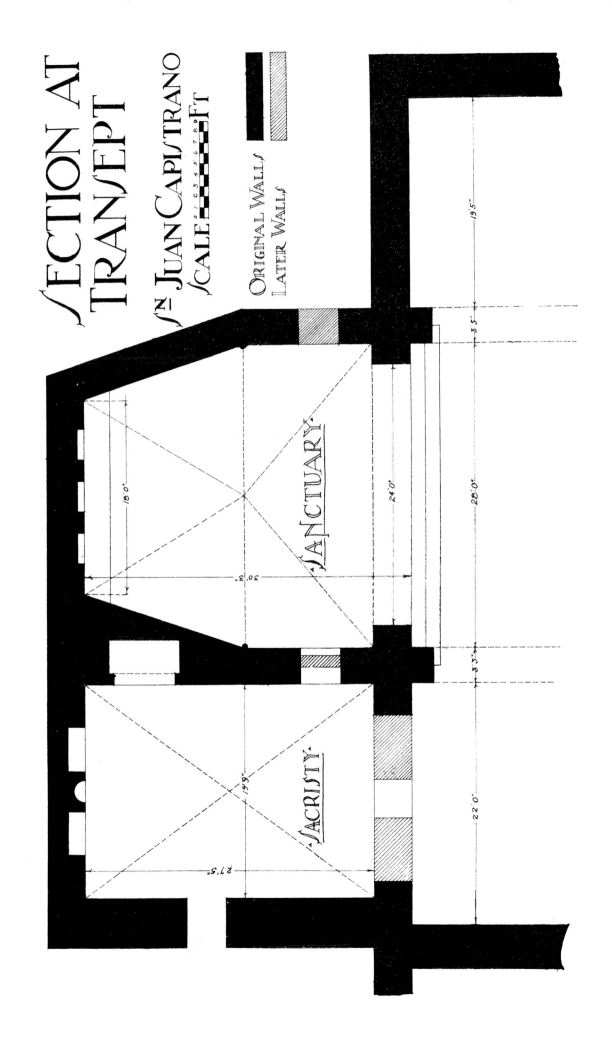

SECTION AT
TRANSEPT
S^N JUAN CAPISTRANO
SCALE 0 1 2 3 4 5 6 7 8 9 FT

ORIGINAL WALLS
LATER WALLS

SANCTUARY·

·SACRISTY·

PLATE 26

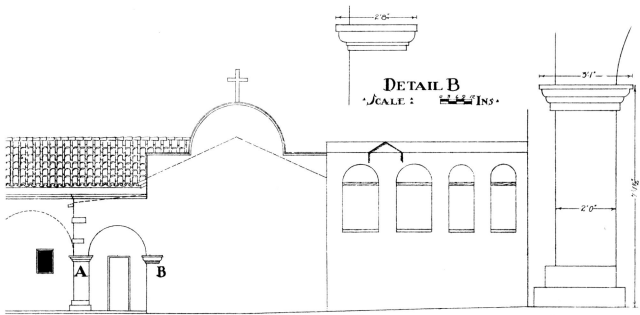

2'8"

DETAIL B
SCALE : 0 3 6 9 12 INS

3'1"

2'0"

CHAPEL·AND·BELFRY·
·SAN·JUAN·CAPISTRANO·

A   B

DETAIL A
SCALE 0 3 6 9 12 INS

·MATERIAL·BRICK·

SCALE FT·

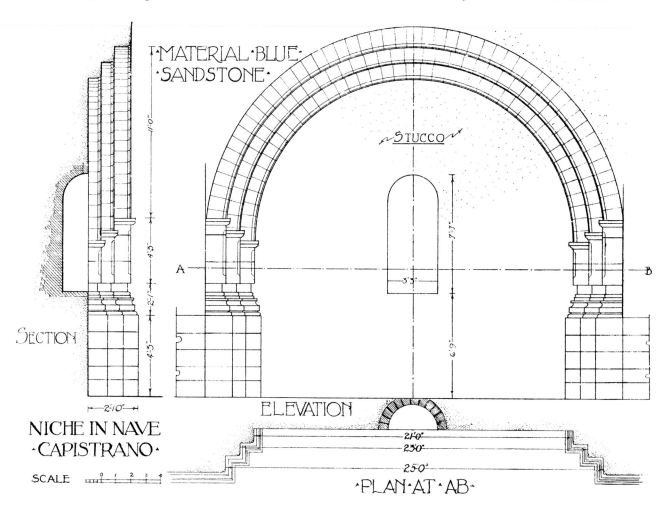

·MATERIAL·BLUE·
·SANDSTONE·

STUCCO

11'0"

4'3"

2'1"

4'3"

A   B

7'3"

3'3"

6'9"

SECTION

2'10"

ELEVATION

NICHE IN NAVE
·CAPISTRANO·

SCALE   0 1 2 3 4

21'0"
23'0"
25'0"

·PLAN·AT·AB·

PLATE 27

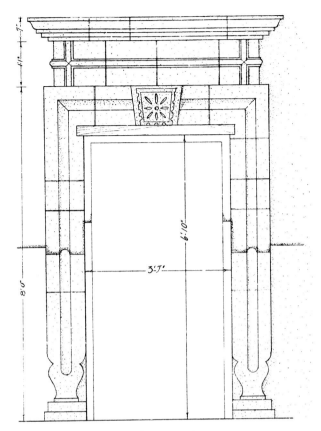

· PRIESTS · HOUSE · CAPISTRANO ·

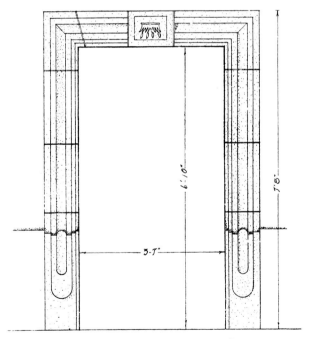

· SACRISTY · CAPISTRANO ·

· MISSION · DOORWAYS ·

MATERIAL · STONE

SCALE ⌐ Ft

PLATE 28

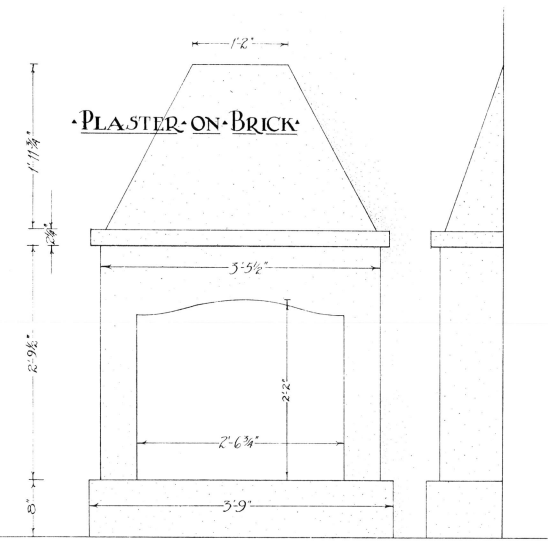

·PLASTER·ON·BRICK·

1'·2"

1'·11¾"

2¼"

2'·9½"

8"

3'·5½"

2'·2"

2'·6¾"

3'·9"

·FIREPLACE·
·SAN·JUAN·CAPISTRANO·
SCALE : 6 3 0 1 2 FT

PLATE 29

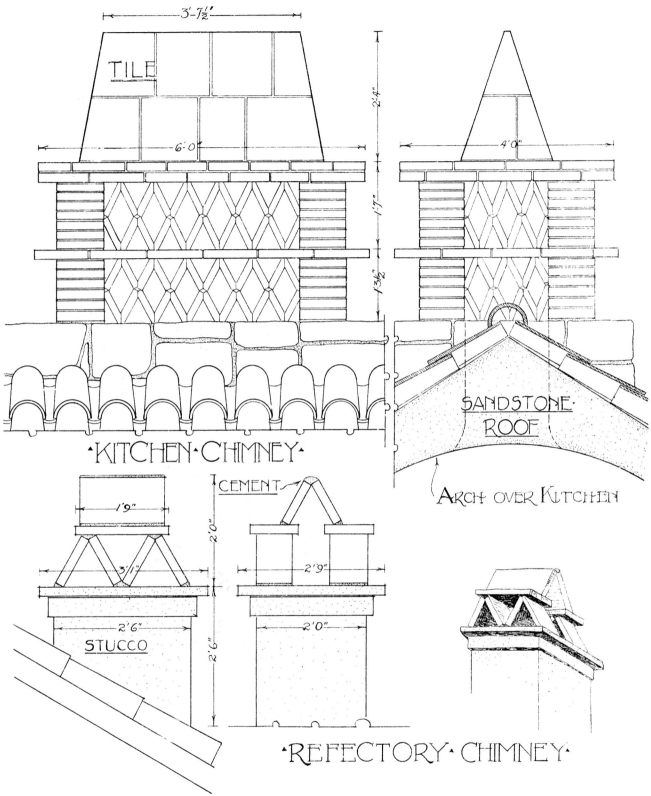

3'-7½"

TILE

2'-4"

6'-0"

1'-7"

13½"

·KITCHEN·CHIMNEY·

4'0"

SANDSTONE·
ROOF

ARCH OVER KITCHEN

CEMENT

1'9"

2'0"

3'1"

2'9"

STUCCO

2'6"

2'0"

2'6"

·REFECTORY·CHIMNEY·

·CHIMNEYS·SAN·JUAN·CAPISTRANO·
·MATERIAL: RED TILES·   ·SCALE   1   2 FT

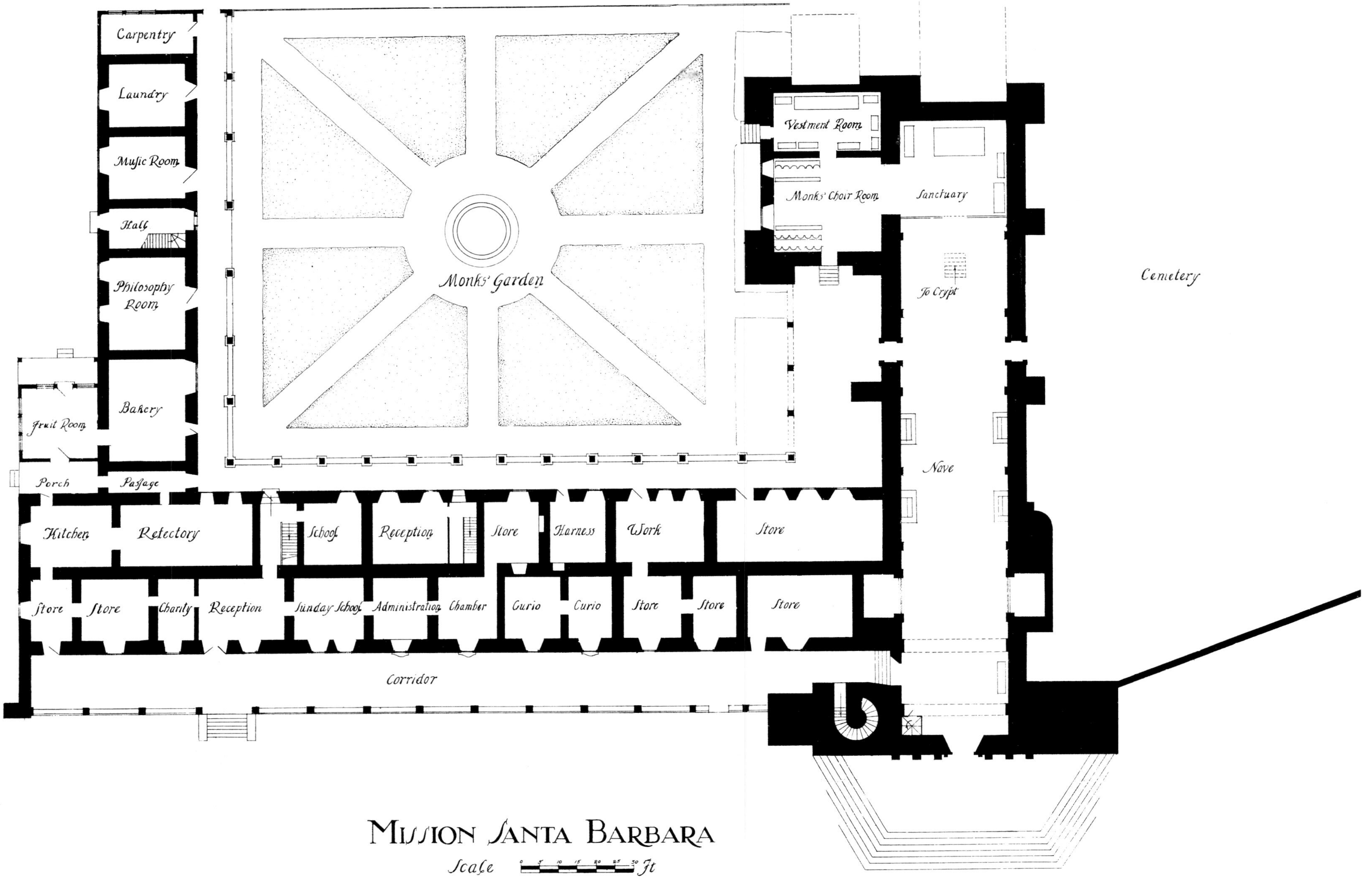

PLATE 30

Cemetery

Sanctuary

To Crypt

Nave

Vestment Room

Monks' Choir Room

Monks' Garden

Carpentry

Laundry

Music Room

Hall

Philosophy Room

Bakery

Fruit Room

Porch

Passage

Refectory

School

Reception

Store

Harness

Work

Store

Store

Kitchen

Charity

Reception

Sunday School

Administration

Chamber

Curio

Curio

Store

Store

Store

Store

Store

Store

Corridor

MISSION SANTA BARBARA

Scale 0 5 10 15 20 25 30 Ft

PLATE 31

Santa Barbara—Façade

PLATE 32

Santa Barbara—Corridor

PLATE 33

Santa Barbara—Monks' Garden

PLATE 34

Santa Barbara—Façade and Fountain

PLATE 35

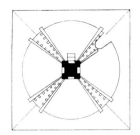

·Plan·at·A·B·

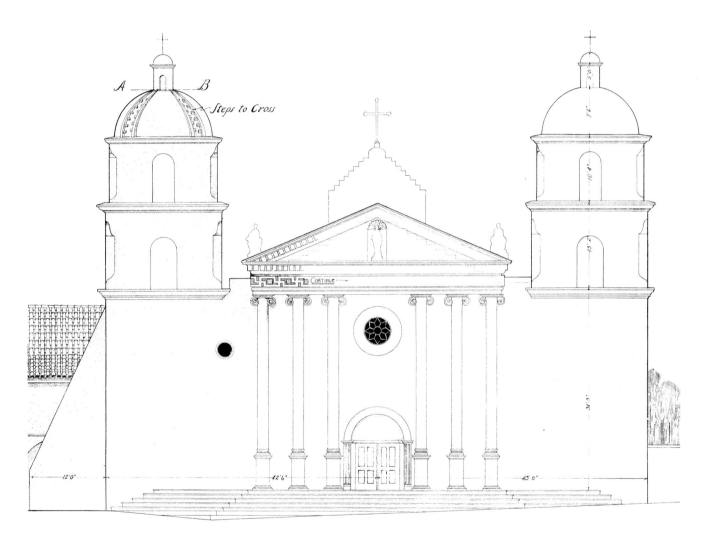

·MISSION · SANTA · BARBARA·

Scale ══════ Ft

PLATE 36

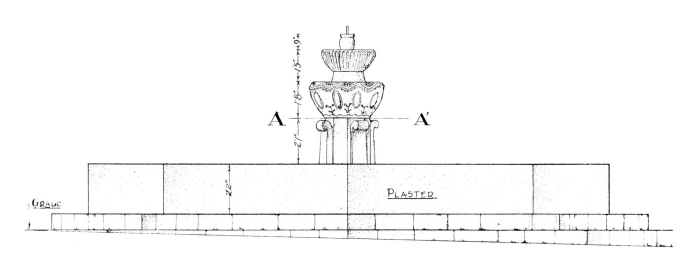

ELEVATION

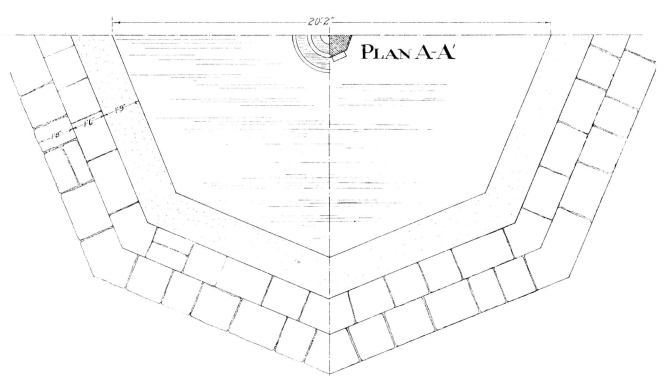

PLAN A-A'

·FOUNTAIN · STA·BARBARA·

·MATERIAL ·STONE·   ·SCALE ⊢⊢⊢⊢⊣FT·

PLATE 37

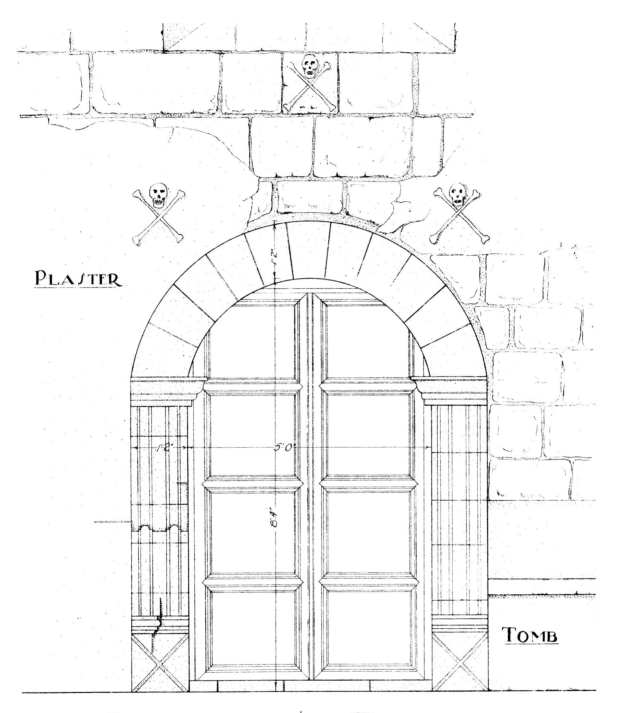

·DOORWAY · STA·BARBARA·

·MATERIAL·STONE·   **·SCALE** FT·

PLATE 38

·CEMETERY· GATEWAY· STA·BARBARA·

·SCALE ▪▪▪▪ 5 FT·   ·MATERIAL ·STONE·

PLASTER

2'3"
4'9"
7'0"
10'10"
7'5"
6'1"
6'2"
4'0"

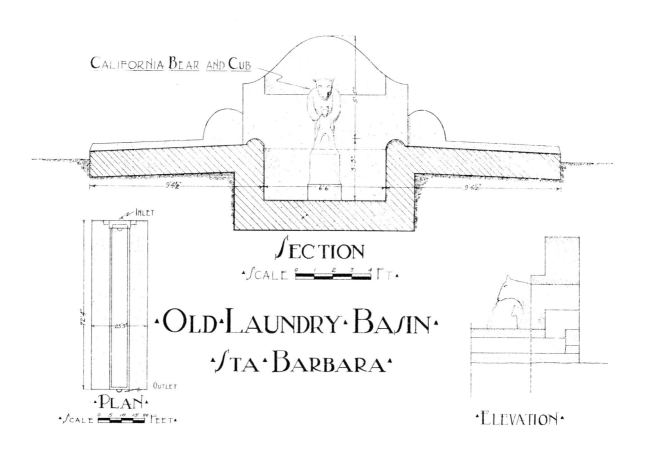

CALIFORNIA BEAR AND CUB

SECTION

·SCALE 0 1 2 3 4 FT·

9'4½"   6'6"   9'4½"
5'5½"
5'5"

INLET

72'4"
25'3"

OUTLET

·PLAN·

·SCALE 0 5 10 15 20 FEET·

·OLD·LAUNDRY·BASIN·

·STA·BARBARA·

·ELEVATION·

PLATE 39

·WINDOW·STA·BARBARA·

·MATERIAL·STONE· ·SCALE·FT·

PLATE 40

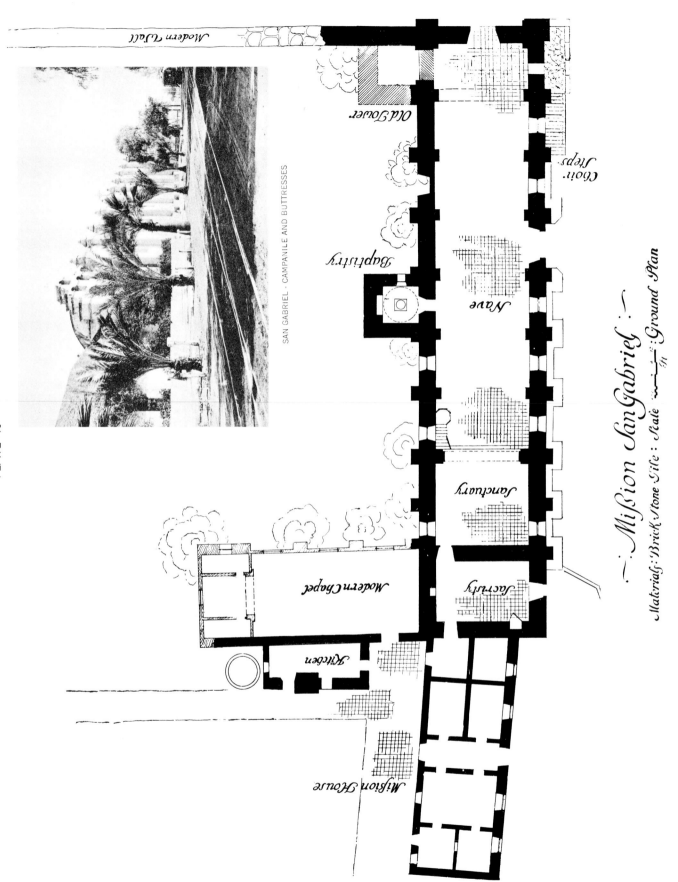

SAN GABRIEL · CAMPANILE AND BUTTRESSES

Modern Wall

Old Tower

Choir Steps

Baptistry

Nave

Sanctuary

Sacristy

Modern Chapel

Kitchen

Mission House

:~ Mission San Gabriel :~

Materials: Brick Stone Tile : Scale |——| Ground Plan

PLATE 41

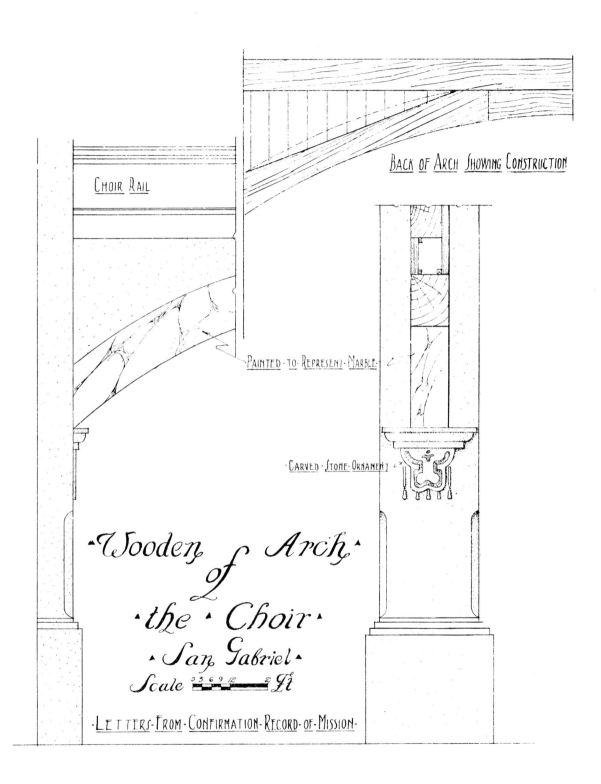

BACK OF ARCH SHOWING CONSTRUCTION

CHOIR RAIL

PAINTED·TO·REPRESENT·MARBLE·

CARVED·STONE·ORNAMENT

·Wooden of Arch·
of
·the·Choir·
·San Gabriel·
Scale ²³⁶⁹¹²   ²Ft

·LETTERS·FROM·CONFIRMATION·RECORD·OF·MISSION·

PLATE 42

San Gabriel—Campanile

PLATE 43

Vault over Sacristy

Cloister

Garden
Wall

Campanile
~ Mission San Gabriel ~
Material: Brick and Stone   Scale: Ft

PLATE 44

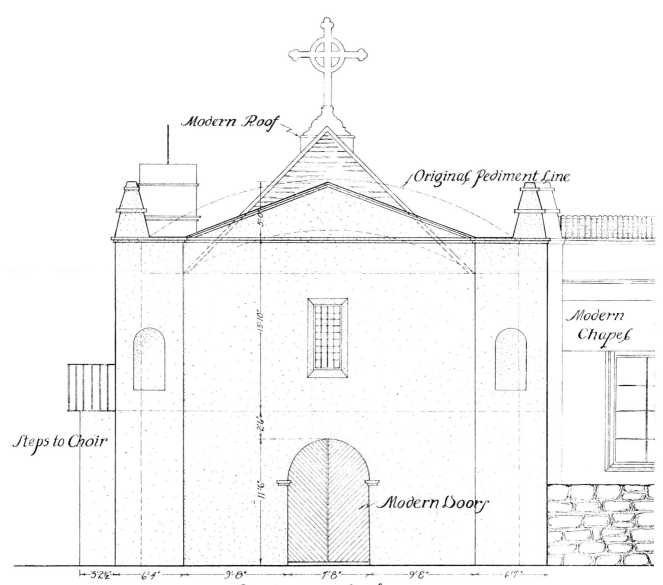

Modern Roof

Original Pediment Line

Modern Chapel

Steps to Choir

Modern Doors

3'2½" · 6'4" · 9'8" · 7'8" · 9'8" · 6'7"

·Eastern Fachada·
·Mißion San Gabriel·
Material: Brick and Stone · Scale ▭ 0 1 2 3 4 5 6 7 8 9 10 11 12 Ft·

PLATE 45

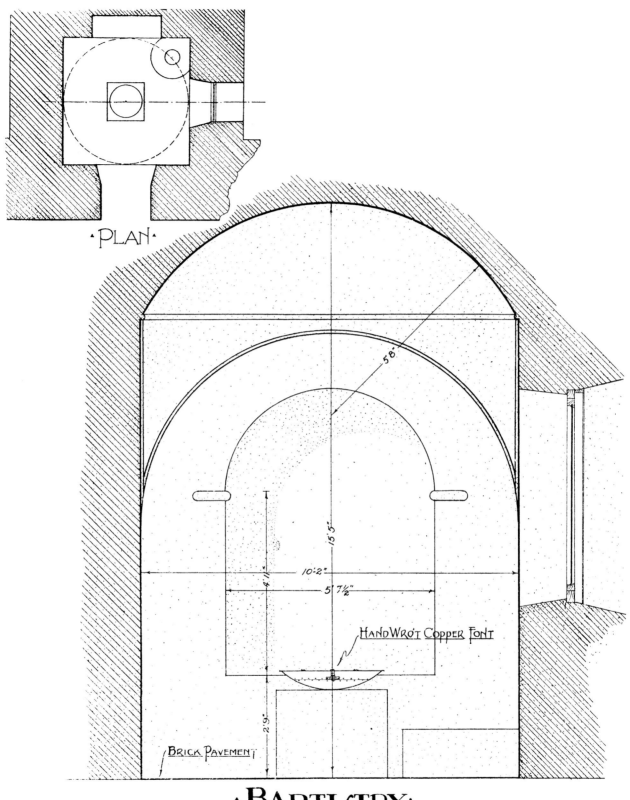

·PLAN·

5'8"

15'5"

10'2"

5'7½"

4'11"

HandWro't Copper Font

2'9"

Brick Pavement

·BAPTISTRY·
·San Gabriel·

·MATERIAL· BRICK·
·AND·STONE·

SCALE 29630 FT

PLATE 46

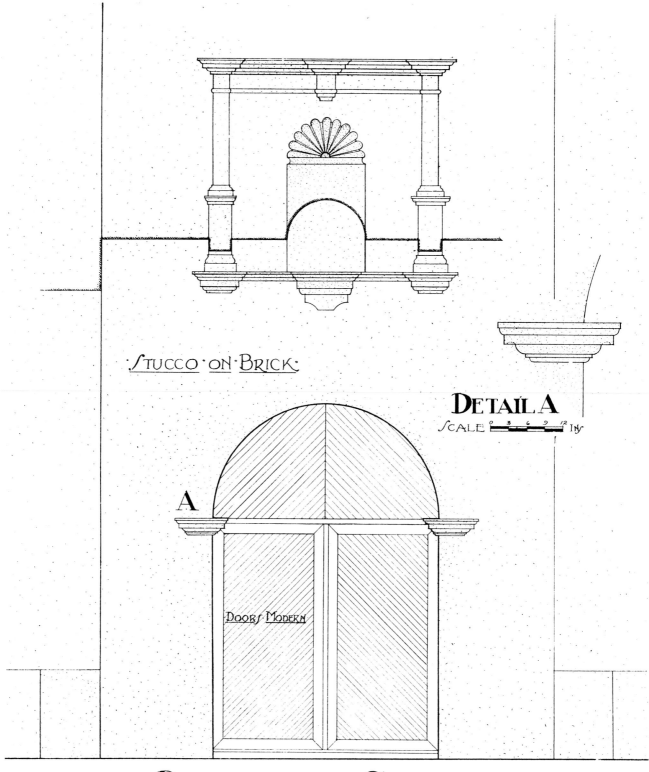

·Stucco·on·Brick·

DETAIL A
SCALE

A

Doors Modern

·Doorway·of·Church·
·San·Gabriel·
SCALE

PLATE 47

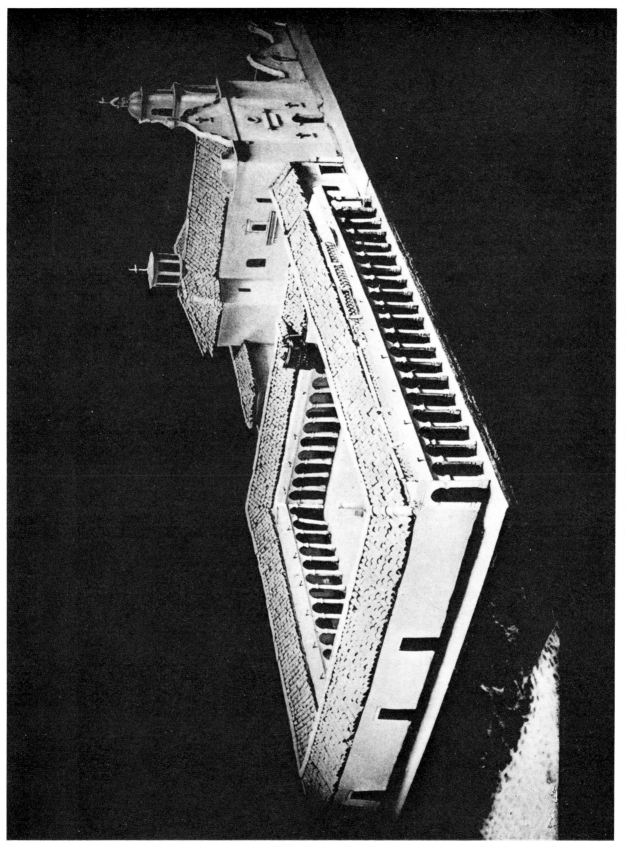

San Luis Rey—Perspective of Model

PLATE 48

San Luis Rey—Façade and Cemetery

PLATE 49

San Luis Rey—Main Portal of Church

PLATE 50

San Luis Rey—Patio before Restoration

PLATE 51

San Luis Rey—Mortuary Chapel

PLATE 52

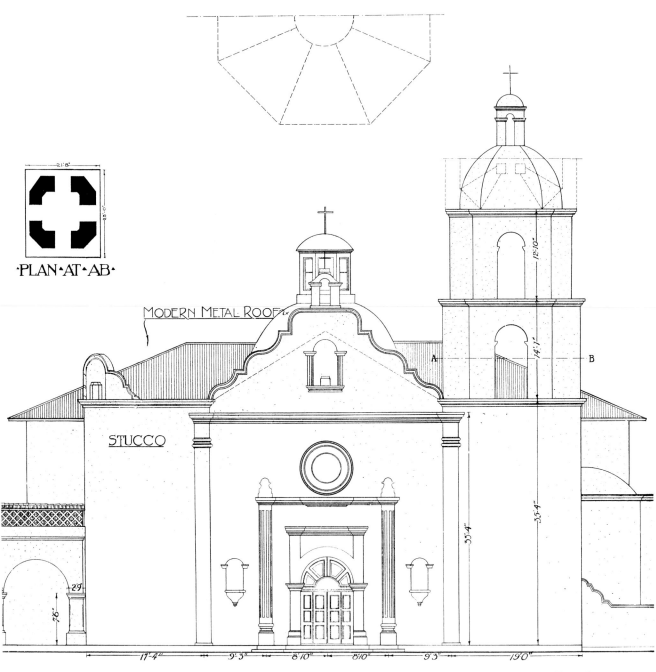

·PLAN·AT·AB·

MODERN METAL ROOF

STUCCO

A · · · B

21'8"

25'-0"

12'-10"

14'-1"

35'-4"

35'-4"

29'

7'6"

17'-4" 9'3" 8'10" 8'10" 9'3" 19'0"

·SCALE·

0 1 2 3 4 5 6 7 8 9 10 11 12 FT·

·FAÇADE·OF·CHURCH·
·MISSION·SAN·LUIS·REY·DE·FRANCIA·

·MATERIAL·
·BRICK·

PLATE 53

·San·Luis·Rey·
·Before·Recent·Restoration·

R·N·1916·

PLATE 54

STUCCO

·DOORWAY·
·Scale· ·San·Luis·Rey· ·Material· Brick·

PLATE 55

DETAIL A
SCALE :

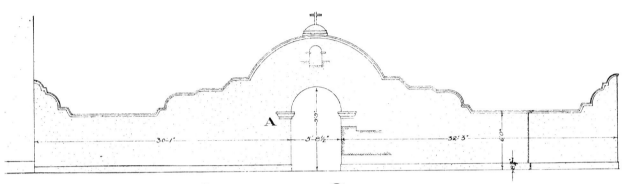

·CEMETERY·GATEWAY·
·MISSION · SAN·LUIS·REY·
·MATERIAL : BRICK STUCCOED ·   ·SCALE :   FT ·

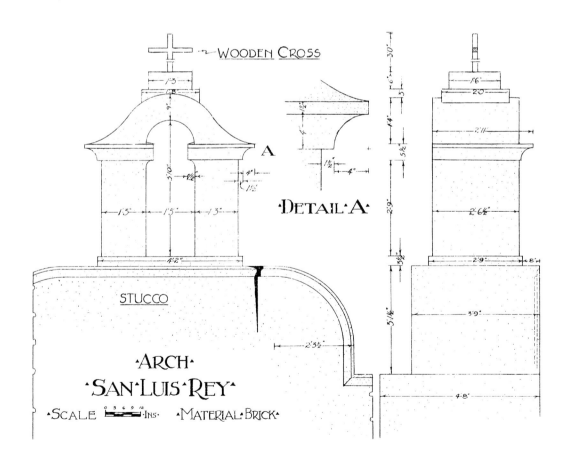

WOODEN CROSS

STUCCO

·ARCH·
·SAN·LUIS·REY·
·SCALE   INS·   ·MATERIAL·BRICK·

DETAIL·A·

PLATE 56

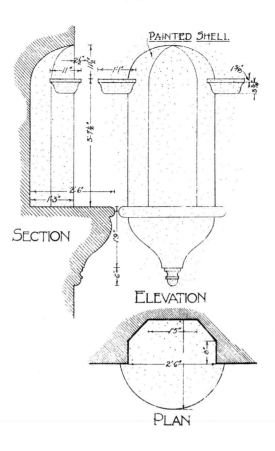

PAINTED SHELL

SECTION

ELEVATION

PLAN

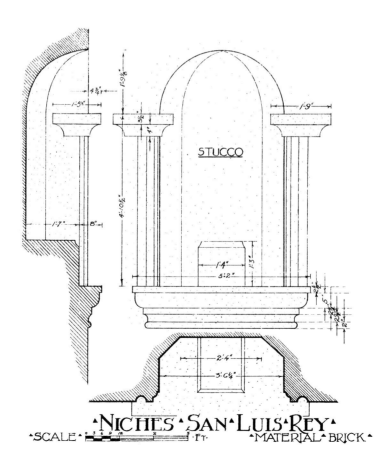

STUCCO

·NICHES·SAN·LUIS·REY·

·SCALE· FT. ·MATERIAL·BRICK·

PLATE 57

San Buenaventura

PLATE 58

San Buenaventura—Side Door / Pala Chapel—Campanile

PLATE 59

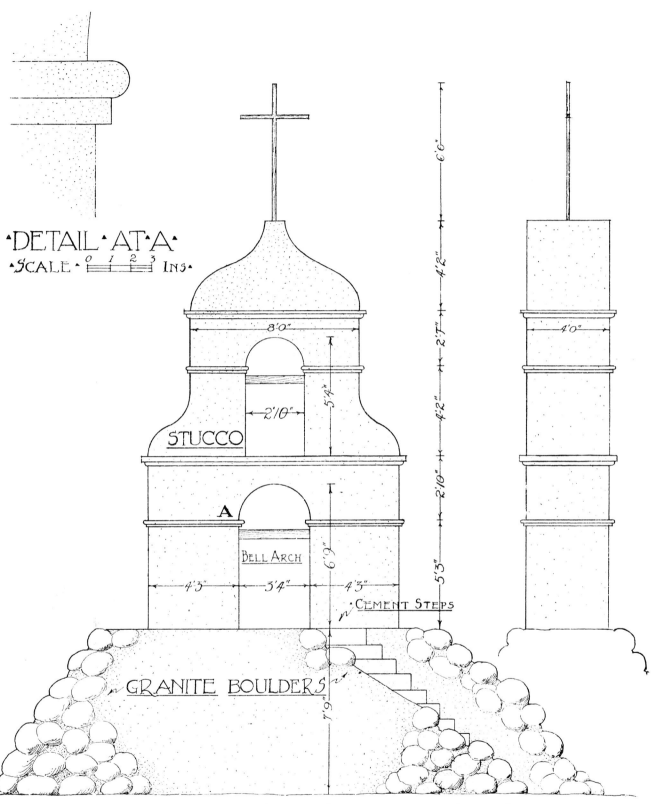

·DETAIL·AT·A·

·SCALE· 0 1 2 3 INS·

8'0"

2'10"

STUCCO

5'4"

A

BELL ARCH

6'9"

4'3"   3'4"   4'3"

CEMENT STEPS

GRANITE BOULDERS

7'9"

6'6"

4'2"

2'7"

4'2"

2'10"

5'3"

4'0"

·CAMPANILE·SAN·ANTONIO·DE·PALA·

·SCALE· 0 1 2 3 4 5 FT· INS·   ·MATERIAL·BRICK·

PLATE 60

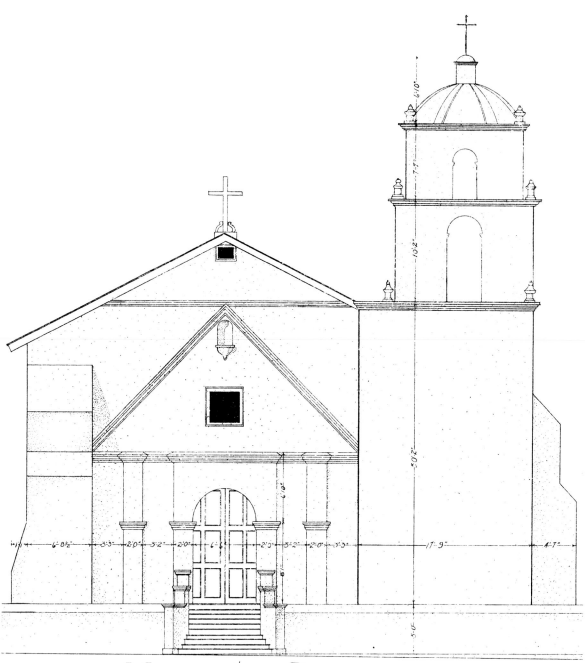

·MISSION · SAN · BUENAVENTURA·

·MATERIAL · ADOBE · BRICK·   ·SCALE ▭▭▭▭ FT·

PLATE 61

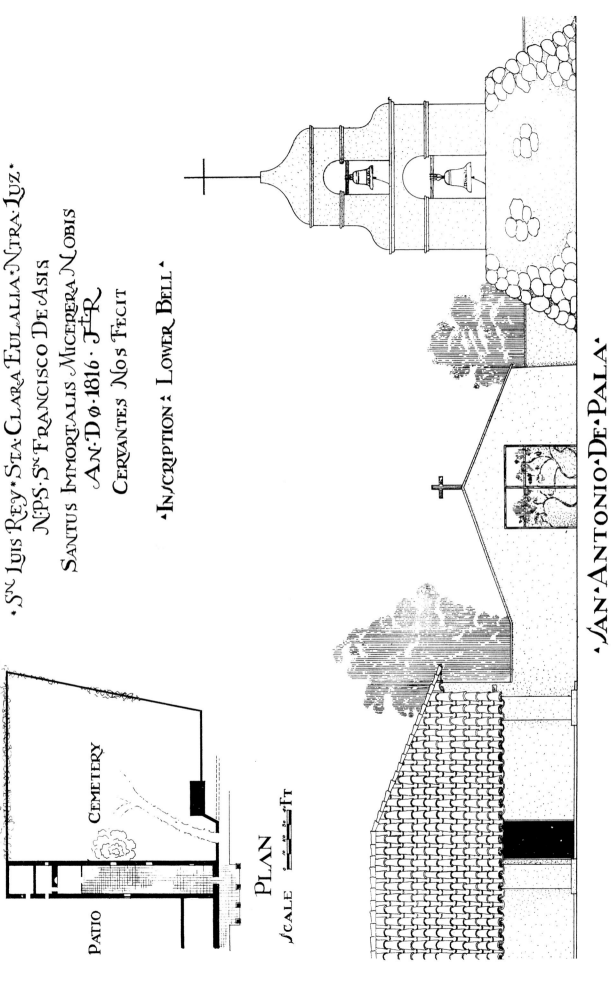

· Sᴺ ·Lᴜɪꜱ· Rᴇʏ · Sᴛᴀ · Cʟᴀʀᴀ · Eᴜʟᴀʟɪᴀ · Nᴛʀᴀ · Lᴜᴢ ·
Nᴘꜱ · Sⁿ · Fʀᴀɴᴄɪꜱᴄᴏ · Dᴇ · Aꜱɪꜱ
Sᴀɴᴛᴜꜱ · Iᴍᴍᴏʀᴛᴀʟɪꜱ · Mɪᴄᴇʀᴇʀᴀ · Nᴏʙɪꜱ
Aɴ · Dᴏ · 1816 · Fʳᴀ ᴿ
Cᴇʀᴠᴀɴᴛᴇꜱ · Nᴏꜱ · Fᴇᴄɪᴛ

· Iɴꜱᴄʀɪᴘᴛɪᴏɴ ᴀ Lᴏᴡᴇʀ · Bᴇʟʟ ·

Cᴇᴍᴇᴛᴇʀʏ

Pᴀᴛɪᴏ

Pʟᴀɴ
Sᴄᴀʟᴇ 0 10 20 30 40 Fᴛ

· Sᴀɴ · Aɴᴛᴏɴɪᴏ · Dᴇ · Pᴀʟᴀ ·

· Sᴀɴ · Aɴᴛᴏɴɪᴏ · Dᴇ · Pᴀʟᴀ ·   Sᴄᴀʟᴇ · Fᴏʀ · Eʟᴇᴠᴀᴛɪᴏɴ 6 4 2 0 2 4 6 Fᴛ ·

· Mᴀᴛᴇʀɪᴀʟꜱ · Bʀɪᴄᴋ ᴀ Aᴅᴏʙᴇ ᴀ Sᴛᴏɴᴇ ·

PLATE 62

San Fernando Rey

PLATE 63

San Fernando Rey—Corridors of Monastery

PLATE 64

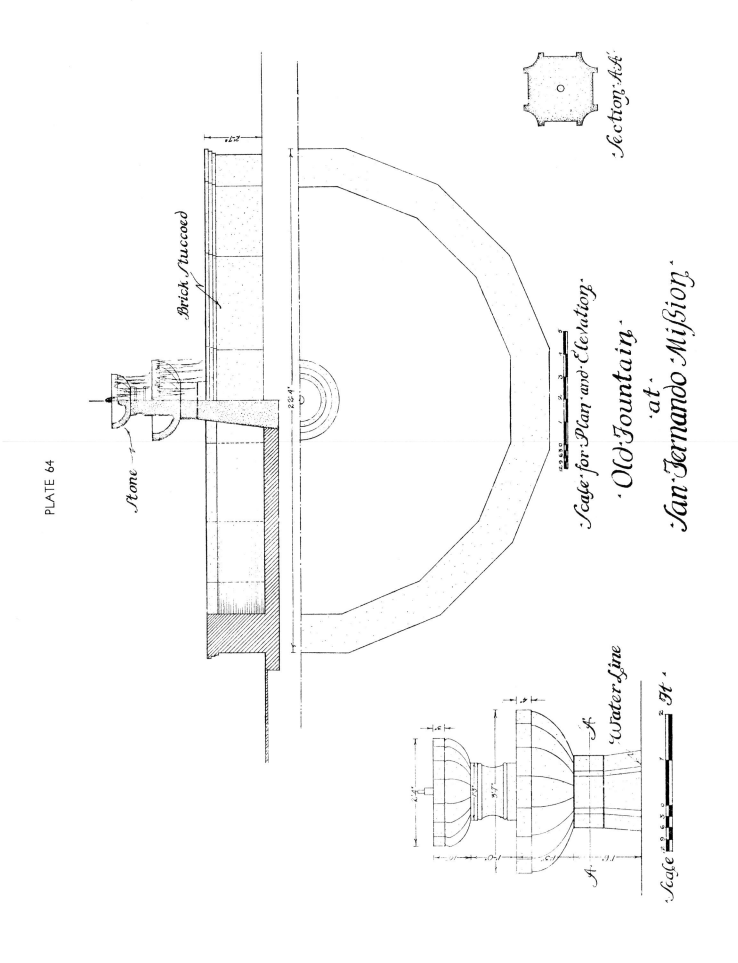

Brick Stuccoed

Stone

Section A.A.

Scale for Plan and Elevation.

Old Fountain
at
San Fernando Mission.

Water Line

Scale

PLATE 65

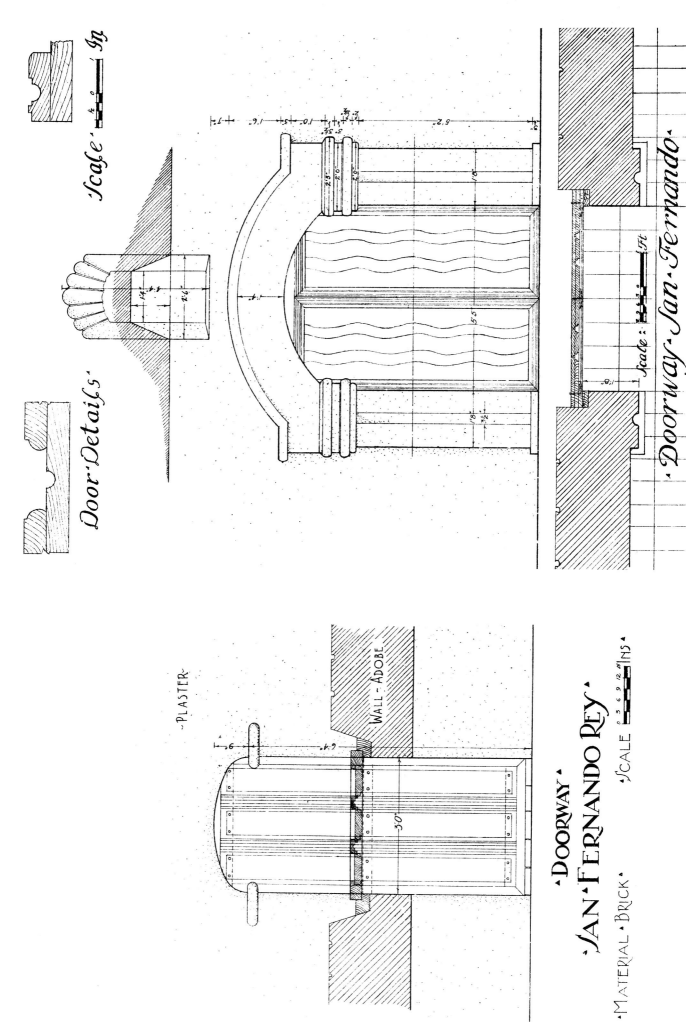

Door·Details·

Scale·¼ʺ = 1ʹ Iꝫ

Doorway·San·Fernando·

~PLASTER~

WALL·ADOBE·

·Doorway·
·San·Fernando Rey·

·Material·Brick·   ·Scale·

PLATE 66

San Francisco (Dolores)—Façade and Interior

PLATE 67

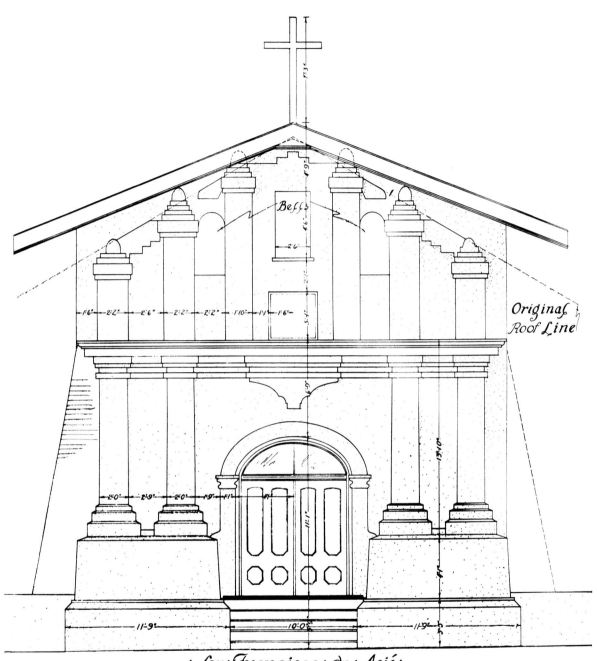

San Francisco de Asis
Material: Adobe and Brick   *Scale ·—————— Ft·*

PLATE 68

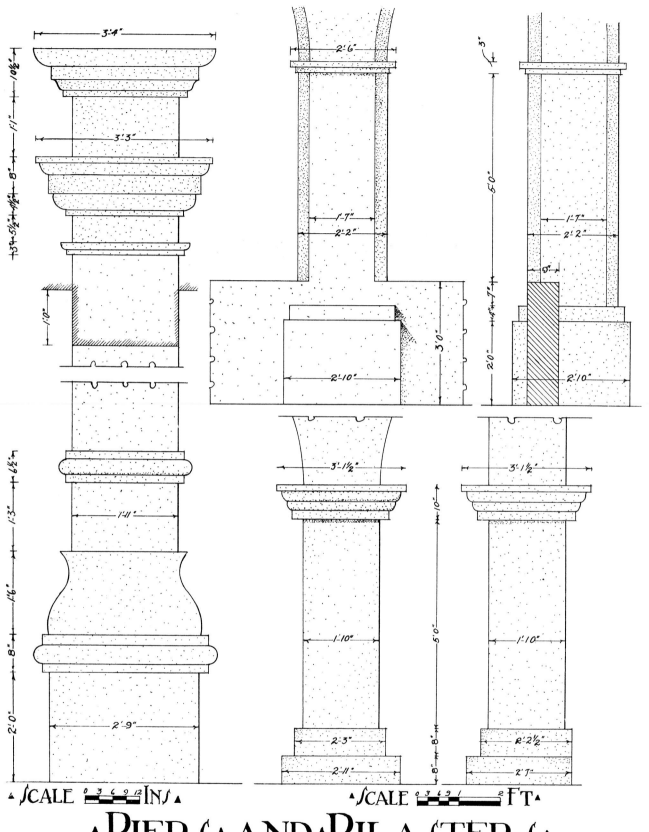

SCALE ⬛▬▬▬ INS

SCALE ⬛▬▬▬ FT

·PIER∫·AND·PILA∫TER∫·
·MATERIAL · BRICK·

PLATE 69

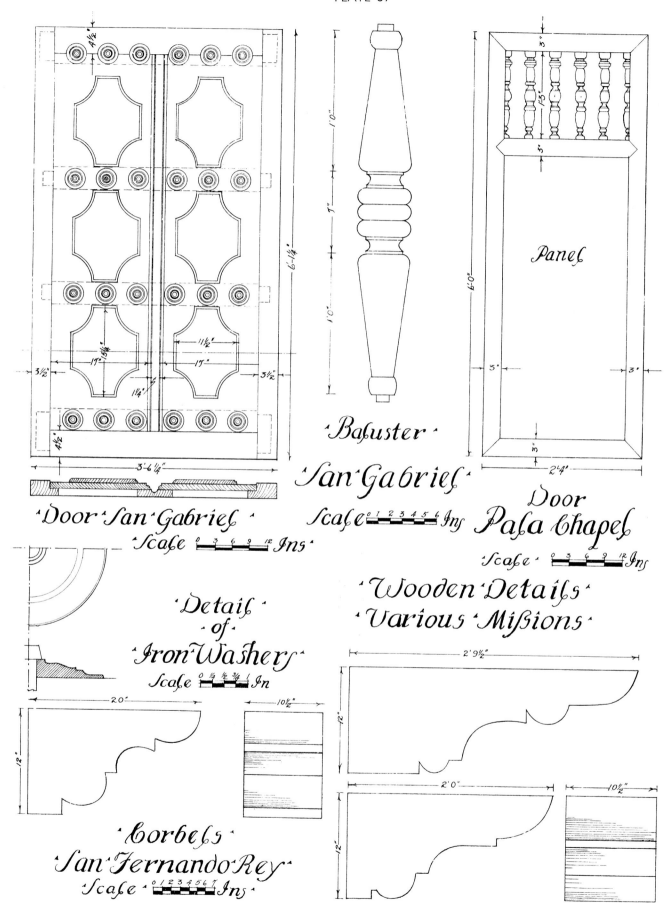

·Door· San· Gabriel ·
·Scale·

·Baluster·

·San·Gabriel·
Scale

Panel

Door
Pala Chapel
Scale

·Wooden·Details·
·Various·Missions·

·Detail·
·of·
·Iron·Washers·
Scale

·Corbels·
·San·Fernando·Rey·
·Scale·

PLATE 70

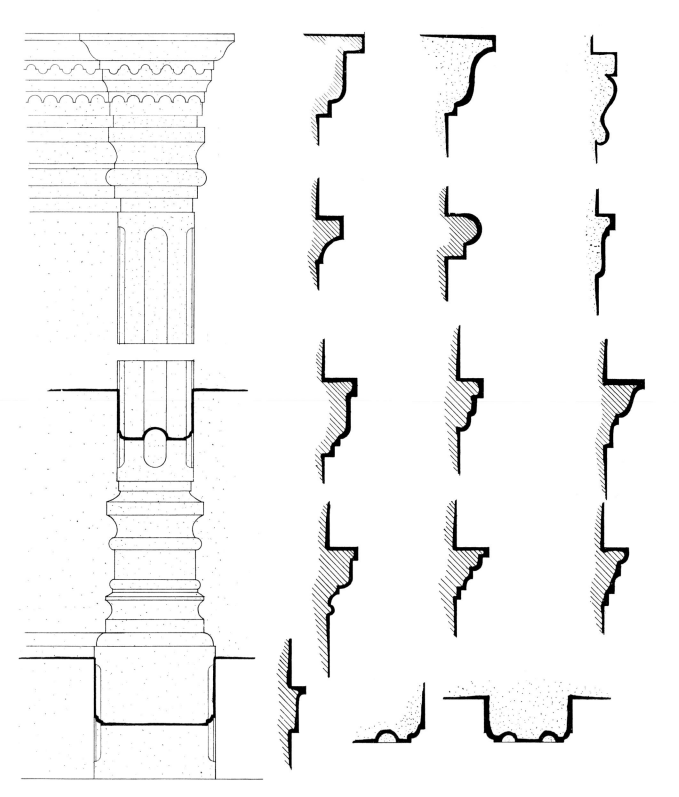

<big>▴ MISSION ▴ MOULDINGS ▴</big>

▴ VARIOUS MATERIALS ▴   ▴ SCALE ═══ FT ▴

PLATE 71

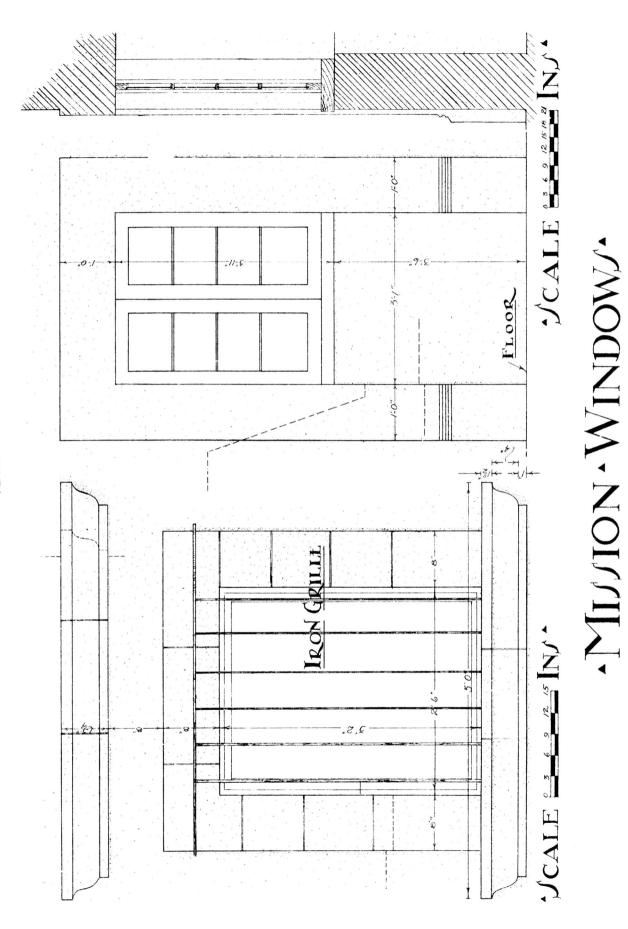

· MISSION · WINDOWS ·

· SCALE · IN · · SCALE · IN · ·

IRON GRILL

FLOOR

PLATE 72

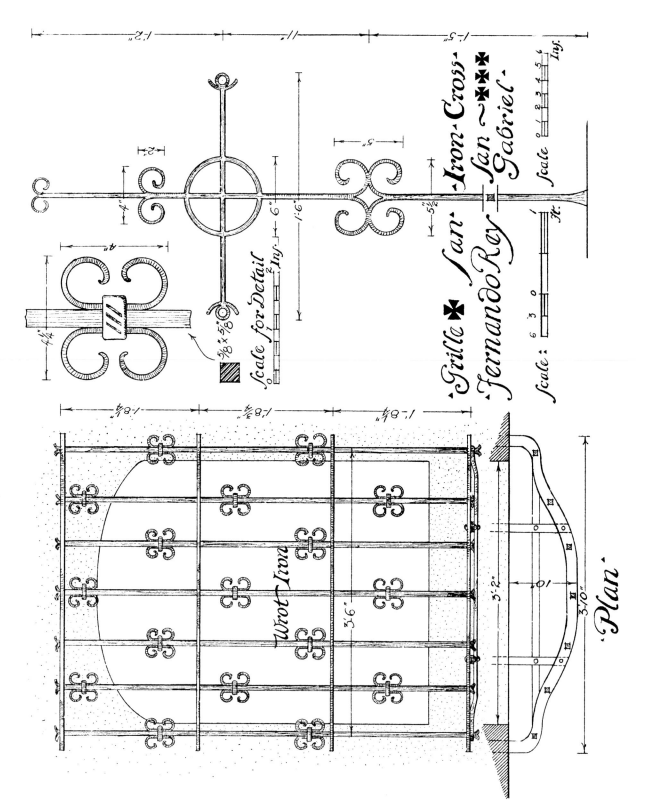

·Grilla· ✠ ·San· ·Iron· Cross·
·Fernando Rey· ~✠✠✠~ ·San·
Gabriel·

Scale for Detail

Wrot Iron

·Plan·

Mission Ironwork

PLATE 73

San Luis Rey

PLATE 74

Santa Clara—Interior

Dover Books on Art

GREEK REVIVAL ARCHITECTURE IN AMERICA, T. Hamlin. A comprehensive study of the American Classical Revival, its regional variations, reasons for its success and eventual decline. Profusely illustrated with photos, sketches, floor plans and sections, displaying the work of almost every important architect of the time. 2 appendices. 39 figures, 94 plates containing 221 photos, 62 architectural designs, drawings, etc. 324-item classified bibliography. Index. xi + 439pp. 5⅜ x 8½.

21148-7 Paperbound $3.50

CREATIVE LITHOGRAPHY AND HOW TO DO IT, Grant Arnold. Written by a man who practiced and taught lithography for many years, this highly useful volume explains all the steps of the lithographic process from tracing the drawings on the stone to printing the lithograph, with helpful hints for solving special problems. Index. 16 reproductions of lithographs. 11 drawings. xv + 214pp. of text. 5⅜ x 8½.

21208-4 Paperbound $2.25

TEACH YOURSELF ANTIQUE COLLECTING, E. Bradford. An excellent, brief guide to collecting British furniture, silver, pictures and prints, pewter, pottery and porcelain, Victoriana, enamels, clocks or other antiques. Much background information difficult to find elsewhere. 15pp. of illus. 215pp. 7 x 4¼.

21368-4 Clothbound $2.00

PAINTING IN THE FAR EAST, L. Binyon. A study of over 1500 years of Oriental art by one of the world's outstanding authorities. The author chooses the most important masters in each period—Wu Tao-tzu, Toba Sojo, Kanaoka, Li Lung-mien, Masanobu, Okio, etc.—and examines the works, schools, and influence of each within their cultural context. 42 photographs. Sources of original works and selected bibliography. Notes including list of principal painters by periods. xx + 297pp. 6⅛ x 9¼.

20520-7 Paperbound $2.50

THE ALPHABET AND ELEMENTS OF LETTERING, F. W. Goudy. A beautifully illustrated volume on the aesthetics of letters and type faces and their history and development. Each plate consists of 15 forms of a single letter with the last plate devoted to the ampersand and the numerals. "A sound guide for all persons engaged in printing or drawing," Saturday Review. 27 full-page plates. 48 additional figures. xii + 131pp. 7⅞ x 10¾.

20792-7 Paperbound $2.25

THE COMPLETE BOOK OF SILK SCREEN PRINTING PRODUCTION, J. I. Biegeleisen. Here is a clear and complete picture of every aspect of silk screen technique and press operation—from individually operated manual presses to modern automatic ones. Unsurpassed as a guidebook for setting up shop, making shop operation more efficient, finding out about latest methods and equipment; or as a textbook for use in teaching, studying, or learning all aspects of the profession. 124 figures. Index. Bibliography. List of Supply Sources. xi + 253pp. 5⅜ x 8½.

21100-2 Paperbound $2.75

LANDSCAPE GARDENING IN JAPAN, Josiah Conder. A detailed picture of Japanese gardening techniques and ideas, the artistic principles incorporated in the Japanese garden, and the religious and ethical concepts at the heart of those principles. Preface. 92 illustrations, plus all 40 full-page plates from the Supplement. Index. xv + 299pp. 8⅜ x 11¼.

21216-5 Paperbound $3.50

DESIGN AND FIGURE CARVING, E. J. Tangerman. "Anyone who can peel a potato can carve," states the author, and in this unusual book he shows you how, covering every stage in detail from very simple exercises working up to museum-quality pieces. Terrific aid for hobbyists, arts and crafts counselors, teachers, those who wish to make reproductions for the commercial market. Appendix: How to Enlarge a Design. Brief bibliography. Index. 1298 figures. x + 289pp. 5⅜ x 8½.

21209-2 Paperbound $2.00

THE STANDARD BOOK OF QUILT MAKING AND COLLECTING, M. Ickis. Even if you are a beginner, you will soon find yourself quilting like an expert, by following these clearly drawn patterns, photographs, and step-by-step instructions. Learn how to plan the quilt, to select the pattern to harmonize with the design and color of the room, to choose materials. Over 40 full-size patterns. Index. 483 illustrations. One color plate. xi + 276pp. 6¾ x 9½.

20582-7 Paperbound $2.50

LOST EXAMPLES OF COLONIAL ARCHITECTURE, J. M. Howells. This book offers a unique guided tour through America's architectural past, all of which is either no longer in existence or so changed that its original beauty has been destroyed. More than 275 clear photos of old churches, dwelling houses, public buildings, business structures, etc. 245 plates, containing 281 photos and 9 drawings, floorplans, etc. New Index. xvii + 248pp. 7⅞ x 10¾.

21143-6 Paperbound $3.00

A HISTORY OF COSTUME, Carl Köhler. The most reliable and authentic account of the development of dress from ancient times through the 19th century. Based on actual pieces of clothing that have survived, using paintings, statues and other reproductions only where originals no longer exist. Hundreds of illustrations, including detailed patterns for many articles. Highly useful for theatre and movie directors, fashion designers, illustrators, teachers. Edited and augmented by Emma von Sichart. Translated by Alexander K. Dallas. 594 illustrations. 464pp. 5⅛ x 7⅛.

21030-8 Paperbound $3.00

Dover publishes books on commercial art, art history, crafts, design, art classics; also books on music, literature, science, mathematics, puzzles and entertainments, chess, engineering, biology, philosophy, psychology, languages, history, and other fields. For free circulars write to Dept. DA, Dover Publications, Inc., 180 Varick St., New York, N.Y. 10014.